Attention Deficit Disorder

Dr. Alvin Silverstein,

Virginia Silverstein, and

Laura Silverstein Nunn

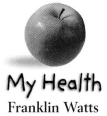

My Health

Franklin Watts

A Division of Grolier Publishing

New York • London • Hong Kong • Sydney

Danbury, Connecticut

Photographs©: Liaison Agency, Inc.: 24 (Dan Nelken), 27 (Stephen Rose), 4 (Sotographs); Peter Arnold Inc.: 35 (Laura Dwight), 22 (Tripos Associates, Inc.); Photo Researchers: 20 right (John Bavosi/SPL), 17 (Loc/Science Source), 19 (Medivisuals/Science Source), 38 (Lawrence Migdale), 20 left (Paul Singh-Roy/SS), 32, 33 (Ellen B. Senisi/Photosynthesis); PhotoEdit: 10 (Tony Freeman), 31 (Michael Newman), 6, 9 (D. Young-Wolff); Photosynthesis: 8, 11, 12, 13, 25, 29 (Ellen B. Senisi); Stock Boston: 16 (Bob Daemmrich), 23 (Spencer Grant), 15 (Dorothy Littell Greco), 26 (Lawrence Migdale); Visuals Unlimited: 18 (Arthur R. Hill).

Cartoons by Rick Stromoski.

Visit Franklin Watts on the Internet at:
http://publishing.grolier.com

Library of Congress Cataloging-in-Publication Data

Silverstein, Alvin.
    Attention deficit disorder / by Alvin Silverstein, Virginia Silverstein, and Laura Silverstein Nunn.
        p. cm.—(My Health)
    Includes bibliographical references and index.
    Summary: Explains what attention deficit disorder is, what causes it, and how it is treated.
        ISBN 0-531-11778-2 (lib. bdg.)   0-531-13967-0 (pbk.)
        1. Attention-deficit—hyperactivity disorder—Juvenile literature.
[1. Attention-deficit-hyperactivity disorder.] I. Silverstein, Virginia B. II. Nunn, Laura Silverstein. III. Title. IV. Series.
RJ506.H9 56   2001
618.92'8589—dc21   00-027345

Printed in the United States of America
1 2 3 4 5 6 7 8 9 10 R 10 09 08 07 06 05 04 03 02 01

Contents

Out of Control 5

Who Gets ADD? 8

What's ADD All About? 10

What Causes ADD? 18

Diagnosing ADD 24

Treating ADD 31

What You Can Do 37

Glossary 40

Learning More 43

Index 46

Out of Control

Are you full of energy and always on the go? Do you have problems sitting still? When you want something, do you need to have it *right now*? Do you call out answers in class and never wait your turn?

Do you have trouble finishing your homework or chores because you are easily **distracted**? Does your mind constantly switch from one idea to another? Is it hard for you to focus for long on just one thing?

If all this describes you or someone you know, you or your friend might have **attention deficit disorder**—or you might not. After all, most children are full of energy and easily distracted. They often act on **impulse**, without thinking. So sometimes it's hard to tell whether a child has attention deficit disorder. This condition is also known by its initials—**ADD**. It used to be called **hyperactivity**.

◀ All kids love to run around and have fun. It's a natural part of being young.

Did You Know...

The word *hyper* means "too much." A hyperactive child is much more active than most kids. He or she usually has trouble sitting still. Hyperactive kids often fidget, rock back and forth, or suddenly jump up and run around.

Not all children with ADD are hyperactive. Some are quiet and dreamy. Instead of paying attention to what is going on around them, they get lost in their own daydreams. They do not cause the same kinds of problems at home and in school that hyperactive kids do, but they have problems of their own.

What could this girl be thinking about? Chances are, it's not schoolwork.

Kids with ADD, whether they are hyperactive or quiet, have a hard time controlling their behavior. They usually do not know when they are getting out of control so they may have a trouble learning in school, behaving at home, or making and keeping friends.

If you or someone you know has ADD, there are things you can do. Some treatments can help, and kids with ADD can learn to control their behavior better. Read on to find out more about ADD.

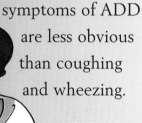

Did You Know...

ADD affects millions of people—teenagers and adults as well as children. Some doctors consider ADD a disease, like asthma. The difference is that the symptoms of ADD are less obvious than coughing and wheezing.

Who Gets ADD?

For many years, scientists believed that only children get attention deficit disorder. They thought kids just "grow out of it" before they become adults. Recent studies have shown that this is not always true. About 3 to 5 percent of kids in the United States have attention deficit disorder. As many as half of these children will continue to have ADD symptoms when they grow up.

Adults with ADD are not usually hyperactive. That may be why doctors used to think that kids grow out of it. Adults with ADD often have trouble paying attention and may act quickly, without thinking. They may also have trouble with relationships and have a hard time finishing projects. Some have low **self-esteem** because they have trouble controlling their behavior.

This 7-year-old girl has ADD.

8

Children as young as 3 years old may show symptoms of ADD, but their parents may think they just have a lot of energy. The symptoms are likely to be noticed around school age, when kids are expected to follow rules and control their behavior.

People with ADD often have family members—parents, grandparents, aunts, uncles, brothers or sisters, or cousins—who also have ADD. If one identical twin has ADD, the other twin is very likely to have it too.

What's ADD All About?

A person with attention deficit disorder may have trouble controlling his or her behavior in different settings, such as at home or in school. Not all kids with ADD behave the same way, however. In fact, ADD symptoms can vary a great deal.

You know you're not supposed to jump on the furniture! Acting out of control can be a sign of ADD.

ADD or ADHD

You may have heard people talking about ADD, but doctors use a different name to describe this condition. They call it **attention deficit hyperactivity disorder** or **ADHD**. Doctors think this name is a better way of describing the different forms this condition may take.

This boy has ADD, also known as ADHD. He is too distracted to concentrate on his homework.

Some children with ADD are full of energy and can't sit still. Others are calm, but they can't concentrate and have trouble paying attention. That's why doctors often talk about three kinds of ADD—**inattentive type**, **hyperactive-impulsive type**, and **combined type.**

Kids with the inattentive type of ADD have trouble paying attention. Their minds are often filled with so many thoughts and ideas that it's hard for them to concentrate on any one thing. They may have trouble learning in class because they are too busy daydreaming. Because these children have a hard time focusing, they often make careless mistakes and have trouble finishing projects. They also find it hard to keep track of things and become distracted easily.

Children with the hyperactive-impulsive type of ADD are full of energy and always on the go. Hyperactive kids are often fidgety and squirm in their seats. They may run around or jump and climb when they are supposed to be sitting still. They may talk constantly too. Impulsive kids

A kid who clowns around in class a lot could be showing signs of ADD.

can't wait their turn. They often speak before they think, and they frequently interrupt other people.

Some kids with ADD have the combined type of ADD. They show both inattentive and hyperactive-impulsive symptoms. They are easily distracted and have trouble finishing projects. They are also fidgety and impulsive. Their behavior may change from day to day—they may be quiet and dreamy one day and bubbling over with energy the next.

This 6-year-old boy is being treated for the combined type of ADD.

Activity 1:
What's It Like to Have ADD?

If you don't have ADD, try to imagine what it feels like. First, turn on the TV and the radio. Then ask a friend to talk to you. While all this is going on, sit down and try to do your homework. Can you tune out all the distractions and do your homework? Can you talk to your friend without paying attention to the TV or radio? Some people with ADD have trouble focusing on just one thing at a time and tuning out the rest.

It's not easy to deal with people who have ADD. Can you imagine trying to talk to someone who acts like a space cadet and doesn't seem to listen to you? Do you have a friend who can't wait for his or her turn when you're playing a game? Sometimes it seems like people with

ADD are unfriendly, strange, too talkative, or mean. That's why some kids with ADD have trouble making and keeping friends. They are often fun to be around because they have a lot of imaginative ideas and a great sense of humor, but it can be hard to spend a lot of time with them.

It's not always easy being friends with some- one with ADD.

Kids with ADD may also have trouble getting along with their own family. They may not listen to their parents, or they may fight with their brothers and sisters all the time. Eventually, kids with ADD may feel as

ADD Superstars

If you have ADD, you may think you are bad or lazy or stupid, but that is not true. Many people with ADD are very smart and creative. You might be surprised to learn that people with ADD have become teachers, doctors, lawyers, movie stars, company presidents, or athletes. Some of the most important and inventive people in history had ADD. For example, some medical experts believe that Benjamin Franklin and Thomas Edison both had ADD.

Some experts believe that Thomas Edison, who was a great inventor and a brilliant man, may have had ADD.

though they can no longer relate to the people in their lives. This can make them feel sad and lonely. They don't feel good about themselves, and they may develop low self-esteem.

What Causes ADD?

Scientists have learned a lot about ADD in recent years. They know that it is not caused by poor parenting or bad teachers. Many people think that eating a lot of sugar can make kids hyperactive, but scientists have learned that most cases of ADD are not caused by a high-sugar diet. Most experts believe that ADD occurs when part of a person's brain doesn't work quite right.

If you ate all this candy, you might get hyper for a little while, but candy doesn't cause ADD.

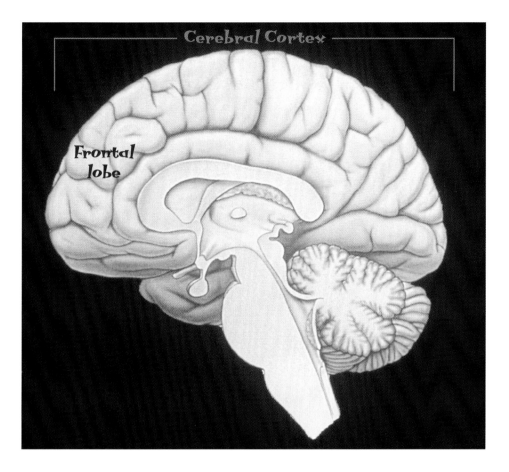

Cerebral Cortex

Frontal lobe

Each part of your brain has a special job to do. The outermost layer of your brain is called the **cerebral cortex**. You use it to think, remember, and make decisions. You also use it to understand and form words and to control body movements. The cerebral cortex receives messages from your ears, eyes, nose, taste buds, and skin and lets you know what is going on in the world around you.

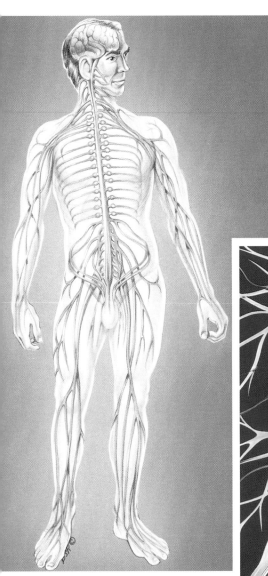

Deeper inside the brain there is a kind of relay station that contains billions of nerve cells. These nerve cells receive messages from all over your body and send out messages that control body activities. Chemicals called **neuro-transmitters** help carry these messages from one part of the brain to

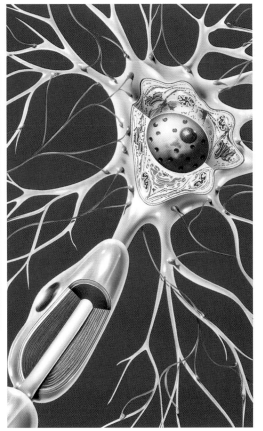

A network of nerves connects the brain and spinal cord with all parts of the body (top left). The branches of a nerve cell (left) pick up messages from other nerve cells and send them on to the next nerve cell in the chain. Eventually, the message reaches the brain.

another. Whenever you concentrate on something—whether it's homework or playing catch with your friends—nerve cells fire off messages back and forth at very high speeds. This fast-paced action makes it possible for you to block out distractions and focus on what you are doing.

The part of the brain right behind your forehead is called the **frontal lobe**. It helps you pay attention, focus on one thing at a time, make plans and stick to them, and think before you act. In many people with ADD, some structures in the frontal lobe of the brain are smaller than usual. As a result, the nerve cells in this area can't pick up enough of an important neurotransmitter known as **dopamine**. At the same time, some nerve cells grab dopamine before it reaches the places where it is needed.

Did You Know...

The frontal lobe of the brain has nothing to do with intelligence. Many smart, creative people have ADD.

$E = Mc^2$

$\sqrt{6,001}$

3.14

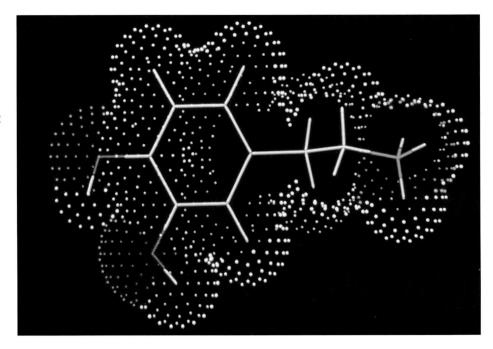

Dopamine helps a person block out distractions and control his or her behavior. When too little dopamine is moving through the brain, a person has trouble focusing on one thing. Some people may also have trouble controlling their actions. That's what happens to many people with ADD.

You can't "catch" ADD the way you can catch a cold, and it is not caused by the way your parents raised you. ADD is usually an **inherited** condition. People who have attention deficit disorder were born with it.

A few cases of ADD have been linked to other possible causes. For instance, a woman who drinks alcohol,

"No, thanks. My baby doesn't drink."

- Alcohol can make your baby small. Small babies are more likely to have problems.

- Alcohol can cause birth defects and mental retardation.

This message is a service from Ross Laboratories, the makers of SIMILAC® WITH IRON Infant Formula.

IF YOU ARE PREGNANT

DON'T DRINK

smokes, or takes drugs while she is pregnant may damage the developing brain of the unborn child. But, most of the time, ADD is passed along in the **genes**. Genes are chemicals that carry inherited traits. In people with ADD, the genes that control the way the brain uses dopamine are different from the genes most people have.

Diagnosing ADD

It's not easy to decide whether a child has ADD. After all, most kids are restless at times. So how do you know whether a child has ADD or is just an energetic person?

Unfortunately, there is no sure way to know because the symptoms of ADD are similar to those of many other conditions.

For example, ear infections can affect a child's hearing and make it seem as though he or she is not listening. Allergies or seizures may also cause behaviors that seem like ADD—and so can family problems, a boring teacher, or a learning disability. A child who seems quiet and withdrawn may be suffering from depression rather than ADD. With all these possibilities, deciding whether a child has ADD can be tough. It's very important for doctors to get the **diagnosis** right because different problems need different treatments.

A Learning Link

A teacher is helping this boy, who has ADD, try to figure out math.

Many experts believe there is a strong link between ADD and learning disabilities. Between 40 and 80 percent of people with ADD have trouble learning certain things, such as reading or math. This can happen even when a person is really smart. Many people think that ADD and learning disabilities are the same thing, but they are not! Sometimes it may be hard to tell the difference. It may seem like a child is not paying attention when the real problem is a learning disability. Similarly, children who have trouble focusing their attention may have trouble learning even though they do not have a learning disability.

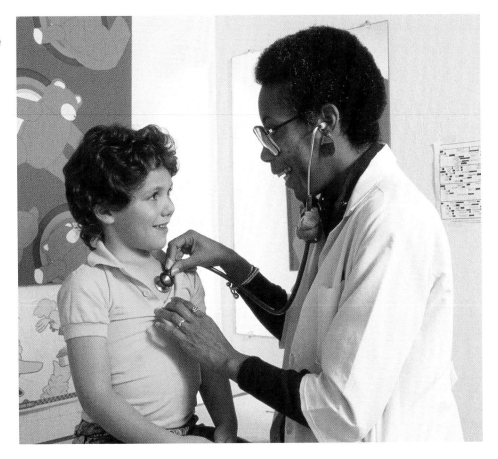

A physical exam is usually a good way to start making a diagnosis. It can rule out other medical problems. The doctor will also ask a lot of questions. Is there any history of medical problems? Does the child get along well with other children? How does he or she behave at home and at school? How long has the child been behaving this way? How often is the child's behavior a problem?

If the doctor thinks the child may have ADD, he or she may suggest that a school counselor see the child. The counselor will ask more questions, looking for examples of inattentive behavior and hyperactive or impulsive behavior. The counselor may also ask the child to take a few tests that can provide a better understanding of his or her problems.

Certain tests can help doctors and counselors decide whether a child has ADD.

☑ Checklist for Diagnosing ADD

Inattentive Type

❏ The child often daydreams in class.

❏ The child is easily distracted.

❏ The child can't remember the teacher's instructions.

❏ The child often loses or forgets his or her homework or books.

❏ The child makes careless mistakes in his or her schoolwork.

❏ The child doesn't listen to his or her parents when they ask him or her to do a task.

❏ The child doesn't stick with a task until it is done.

Hyperactive/Impulsive Type

❏ The child fidgets a lot and can't sit still.

❏ The child blurts out answers in class.

❏ The child interrupts friends while they are speaking.

❏ The child can't wait his or her turn in games or groups.

❏ The child is always "on the go." He or she runs around a lot or climbs up on things when he or she is supposed to be sitting.

❏ The child's mind flows with ideas, and he or she talks constantly.

Everybody does some of these things from time to time. Doctors and counselors will decide that a child has ADD only if he or she shows many of the behaviors listed in the chart on page 28. These behaviors must continue for at least 6 months, and they must appear before the child is 7 years old.

These behaviors must be more serious in a child with ADD, and they must happen more often than in other children of the same age. Also, the behaviors must create major problems in at least two areas of a child's life: school, home, or social settings with friends.

Having problems learning in school could be a sign of ADD.

If a child has problems at school, but behaves normally at home and with friends, he or she probably does not have ADD.

How Common Is ADD?

Would you believe that in the United States at least one child in a class of twenty-five kids is diagnosed with ADD? This is hard to believe, which is why some people think that ADD is being **overdiagnosed**. Medical experts disagree. They say that because scientists have learned a lot about ADD in recent years, doctors are now better able to identify it.

Treating ADD

When most people think about ADD, they also think about **Ritalin**. Ritalin is a medicine used to treat ADD. Many people are frightened by the idea of giving kids a drug that they will take every day for many years. They also think that too many children are being treated with Ritalin. Others think of Ritalin as a "magic pill" that can make ADD seem to disappear. Ritalin can help kids with ADD focus better and control their behavior, but it does not cure ADD.

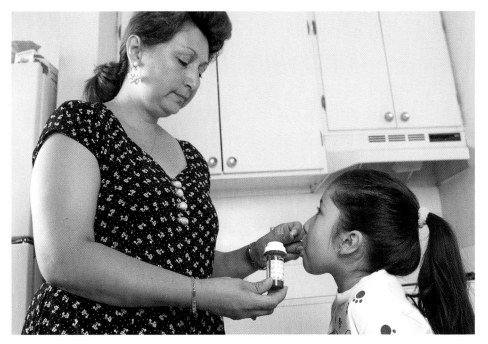

Many kids with ADD need to take medication every single day.

A "Wake-Up Drug" to Calm Down

As many as 80 percent of children with ADD are helped by Ritalin and other ADD medications. These drugs are **stimulants** that usually make people feel more wide awake and full of energy. Some people with sleep problems take Ritalin to stay awake during the day.

Ritalin doesn't make kids with ADD more hyper or active. Instead, it seems to calm them down. It helps them to pay attention and concentrate so they are not as easily distracted. In children with ADD, Ritalin brings brain chemicals back to normal levels.

Thanks to medication, this boy can finally sit down and do his homework without distractions.

For treatment to be successful, children with ADD need the support of their parents, teachers, and counselors. Counselors can help children and family members learn about ADD and how to deal with it. They can also talk to the children about their problems and help them feel better about themselves. They can help to reduce the child's worries and anxieties. They can also teach the child how to handle specific situations at home, at school, or with friends.

Parents and teachers need to learn about ADD so that they can understand what the child is going through. The more they know about ADD, the more they can help kids with these problems. Both parents and teachers can learn ways to change a child's behavior into something more acceptable.

This teacher is helping a boy with ADD. He is trying to learn how to write numbers.

Behavior modification is a technique often used to change a person's behavior. The parent, teacher, or counselor sets goals for a child with ADD. The adult then rewards good behavior and either ignores bad behavior or works with the child to correct it. There are three steps in this process.

1. *Define the problem.* If the problem is restlessness, for example, the child can begin by trying to sit still during dinner.

2. *Set a reasonable goal.* At first, it may be too hard for a child with ADD to sit still until everyone in the family has finished eating. It is a good idea to break up the big goal into little goals that are easier to reach. For instance, the child can try sitting at the table for 5 minutes, then 10 minutes, then 15 minutes.

3. *Work toward the goal.* Kids with ADD respond well to rewards and consequences. Parents, teachers, and friends should praise the child whenever he or she makes some progress, even if the child does not achieve the goal. This will show that they are proud of the child's progress. A parent could say, "I like how nicely you are sitting in your chair and eating your dinner." A great way to reward kids for good behavior is by placing stickers on a chart.

Each time the child does well, he or she receives a sticker.

If the child is working toward a goal, such as sitting through dinner, progress can be marked on the chart. After the child collects a certain number of stickers, he or she will be rewarded with a special treat, such as going to the movies or getting an ice cream cone.

Discipline is also important. Kids with ADD need to know that there are consequences for their behaviors. Many people use time-outs. The child should be told what

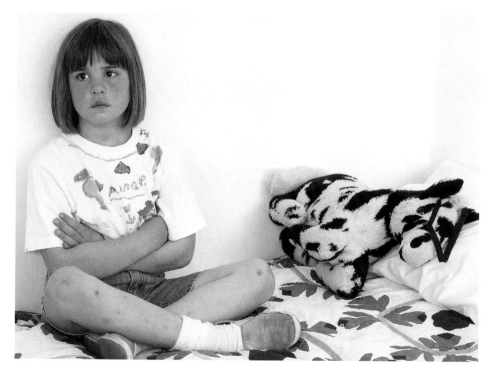

A time-out can help calm down a child who gets out of control.

kind of behavior is not acceptable. If the child does not follow these rules, he or she should be taken to a quiet area to think about the situation. The parent should keep an eye on the child and not talk to him or her until the time is up.

It is very important for parents and teachers to have a lot of patience and understanding. Friends and other family members can help too. Treatment can be a long, frustrating process, but kids with ADD usually try hard to get better.

What You Can Do

If you have ADD, you are probably tired of hearing, "Why can't you sit still?" "Are you listening to me?" or "Did you forget your homework *again*?" You don't mean to get in trouble. By now, you know that it's not your fault that you act the way you do. Hopefully, you are getting help for your condition. Here is a list of some other things you can do to help yourself listen better, remember things better, and get things done.

- Write a note to yourself. Colored Post-it® notes are great because you can stick them anywhere.
- If your mom or dad wants you to do something, tell them to write you a note so that you won't forget.
- Use a calendar to keep track of places you have to go.
- Try to do tasks right away. If you put them off for later, you might forget about them.
- If you have to go somewhere at a certain time, set the kitchen timer. For instance, if you have to go to soccer practice in a half hour, set the timer for 30 minutes.

- When you finish your homework, always put your schoolbooks in the same special place so that you won't have to hunt for them in the morning.
- Before you go to bed, decide what clothes you will wear the next day. That way you won't have to rush around in the morning.
- Develop a morning routine: go to the bathroom, brush your teeth, take a shower, get dressed, eat breakfast, get your books, and go to school.

A morning routine that includes brushing your teeth and eating a healthful breakfast can help you get a good start to your day.

Activity 2: Set Your Own Goals

If you have ADD, make a list of five things that you want to do today. You may want to include doing your homework, cleaning up your room, giving your dog a bath, setting the table for dinner, or other daily chores. Write down how long each activity should take. Put a check mark next to each item after you do it. At the end of the day, look at how many things you got done. How did you do? Each goal that you meet will make you feel proud of yourself. If you find you're having trouble getting things done, maybe you should make a new list every day and keep trying. Eventually, you'll be able to reach all your goals.

Glossary

attention deficit disorder (ADD)—a condition characterized by an inability to concentrate, pay attention, and/or control one's actions. See also attention deficit hyperactivity disorder.

attention deficit hyperactivity disorder (ADHD)—the medical term for attention deficit disorder (ADD)

behavior modification—a treatment often used to change behavior in people with ADD

cerebral cortex—the outermost layer of the brain. We use it to think, remember, make decisions, and control the movements of the body.

combined type—a kind of ADD in which a person shows both inattentive and hyperactive-impulsive symptoms

diagnosis—identifying a medical condition from its symptoms.

distract—to confuse, to have trouble focusing attention on one thing

dopamine—a neurotransmitter chemical that works in the brain to help focus attention

frontal lobe—the part of the brain that helps you concentrate, make plans, and think before you act

gene—a material inside the body that carries information about a person's characteristics

hyperactive-impulsive type—a kind of ADD. A hyperactive person has more energy than most people. An impulsive person acts without thinking.

hyperactivity—having more energy than normal

impulse—a sudden, unexplained action

inattentive type—a kind of ADD in which the person has difficulty paying attention

inherited—passed on by genes from parents to children

neurotransmitter—a chemical that carries messages from one part of the brain to another

overdiagnose—to identify a certain illness more often than it actually occurs

Ritalin—a drug used to treat ADD, especially the hyperactive type

self-esteem—how you feel about yourself

stimulant—a drug that makes most people feel more alert and energetic

Learning More

Books

Ingersoll, Barbara D. *Distant Drums, Different Drummer: A Guide for Young People with ADHD.* Bethesda, MD: Cape Publications, Inc., 1995.

_____. *Daredevils and Daydreamers: New Perspectives on Attention-Deficit Hyperactivity Disorder.* New York: Doubleday, 1998.

Martin, Grant. *The Attention Deficit Child.* Colorado Springs, CO: Chariot Victor Publishing, 1998.

Nadeau, Kathleen G. and Ellen B. Dixon. *Learning to Slow Down and Pay Attention: A Book for Kids About ADD.* Washington, D.C.: Magination Press, 1997.

O'Dell, Nancy E. and Patricia A. Cook. *Stopping Hyperactivity: A New Solution.* Garden City Park, NY: Avery Publishing Group, 1997.

Osman, Betty B. *Learning Disabilities and ADHD.* New York: John Wiley & Sons, Inc., 1997.

Phelan, Thomas W. *All About Attention Deficit Disorder.* Glen Ellyn, IL: Child Management Inc., 1996.

Quinn, Patricia O. and Judith M. Stern, *Putting on the Brakes: Young People's Guide to Understanding Attention Deficit Hyperactivity Disorder (ADHD)*. Washington, D.C.: Magination Press, 1991.

Organizations and Online Sites

ADHD Links
http://www.central.edu/education/REX/sped/addlinks.html
This site features links to various ADHD resources.

Attention Deficit Disorder & ADHD
http://www.helpforadd.com/info.htm
At this site, Dr. David Rabiner provides information and answers questions about ADHD.

Attention Deficit Disorder Association (ADDA)
National Headquarters
1788 Second Street, Suite 200
Highland Park, IL 60035
http://www.add.org
This national organization provides information about ADD. Its website includes a kid's area with lots of information and animated illustrations.

Attention Deficit Hyperactivity Disorder ADD/ADHD
http://www.cdipage/adhd.htm
Visit this site for plenty of practical, up-to-date information from the Child Development Institute.

Children and Adults with Attention-Deficit Disorders (CHADD)

8181 Professional Place, Suite 201
Landover, MD 20785
http://www.chadd.org
This organization provides information to and offers support for people with ADD.

National Institute of Mental Health

5600 Fishers Lane, Room 7C-02
Rockville, MD 20857
http://www.nimh.nih.gov/publicat/adhd.htm
This national center offers an online pamphlet packed with information on attention deficit hyperactivity disorder.

Someone I Know Is Hyperactive

http://kidshealth.org/kid/health_problems/adhdkid.html
This online site provides easy-to-read, straightforward information about ADD.

Index

Activities
  having ADD, 14
  setting goals, 39
ADD. *See* Attention deficit
  disorder
Allergies, 24
Attention deficit disorder
  adults with, 7, 8
  as a disease, 7
  causes of, 18–22
  checklist, 28
  diagnosing, 24–30
  family members with, 9
  high-sugar diet and, 18
  living with, 37–38
  overdiagnosis of, 30
  possible causes of, 22–23
  studies of, 8
  symptoms of, 5, 6, 10, *10,*
  11, 24
  three kinds of, 11
  treatment for, 7, 31–36
Attention deficit hyperactivity
disorder (ADHD). *See* Attention
deficit disorder

Behavior modification, 34–35
  steps of, 34
Brain, 18, 19, 20, 21, 22, 23,
  32

Candy, *18*
Cerebral cortex, 19, *19*
  job of the, 21
Chemicals. *See* neurotransmitters
Children, 5, 6, 8, 9, 11, 26, 32
Chores, 5, 39
Combined type, 11, 13, *13*
Counselor, 27, *27,* 29, 32, 34

Daydreams, 6
Depression, 25
Discipline, 35–36
  time-outs, 35, *35*
Doctors, 7, 8, 11, 17, 25, 26, 27,
  29, 30
Dopamine, 21, 22, *22,* 23

Ear infections, 24
Edison, Thomas, 17, *17*
Energy, 5, 9, 11, 12, 13, 32

Family, 16, *16,* 25, 32, 36
Franklin, Benjamin, 17
Friends, 5, 7, 14, 15, *15,* 21, 29,
   30, 32, 36
Frontal lobe, 21
   job of the, 21

Genes, 23

Home, 6, 7, 26, 29, 30, 32
Homework, 5, *11,* 14, 21, *32,*
   37, 38, 39
Hyperactive, 5, 6, 7, 8, 12, 18,
   27
Hyperactive-impulsive type, 11,
   12, 28

Inattentive type, 11, 28

Learning disability, 25

Nerve cells, 20, *20,* 21
Neurotransmitters, 20, 21

Parents, 9, 22, 32, 33, 34, 36
Physical exam, 26, *26*

Ritalin, 31, 32

School, 6, *6,* 7, *9,* 26, 29, *29,*
   30, 32

Scientists, 8, 18, 30
Seizures, 24
Self-esteem, 8, 17
Stimulants, 32

Teachers, 18, 25, 32, 33, *33,*
   34, 36
Tests, 27, *27*

About the Authors

Dr. Alvin Silverstein is a professor of biology at the College of Staten Island of the City University of New York. **Virginia B. Silverstein** is a translator of Russian scientific literature. The Silversteins first worked together on a research project at the University of Pennsylvania. Since then, they have produced six children and more than 160 published books for young people.

Laura Silverstein Nunn, a graduate of Kean College, has been helping with her parents' books since her high school days. She is the coauthor of more than 30 books on diseases and health, science concepts, endangered species, and pets. Laura lives with her husband Matt and their young son Cory in a rural New Jersey town not far from her childhood home.